AI Query Engineering Guide

Terminology & Procedures
Find Your Way in the AI Industry

Dayle I. Fish

Copyright and ISBN

TOC Table of Contents

Preface

I served in the U.S. Navy and retired after more than 23 years of active duty, working in Naval Command and Control Operations around the world—both aboard ships and on command staffs. I rose to the rank of Master Chief Petty Officer and served as Director of Advanced Operations Specialist Training at Dam Neck, Virginia. It was during my time in Vietnam waters, in 1972 while aboard an NTDS (Naval Tactical Data System) Cruiser, that I first encountered what we would come to call" Digital Warfare".

Following my military service, I continued in the defense sector as a government contractor, performing similar duties at a higher level. I eventually transitioned into software testing, serving for ten years as a Software Test Manager with Northrop Grumman Mission Systems. It was there that we helped develop the renowned Global Command and Control System (GCCS)—a primary decision-support tool for the U.S. military. As a software Test Manager, I oversaw the development of an application that employed middleware to create a GUI for the customer to query Military Cargo Aircraft regarding the types of cargo being transported. This would be my first encounter with the term Query, in 2001. The user would build the Query using a dashboard.

Throughout my entire career, my mission has been singular: to ensure that command decision-makers have access to the most accurate and timely digital data available—often to make life-or-death decisions in real time.

Now, in my 70s, I've approached the emergence of Artificial Intelligence with a profoundly serious interest. This tool is a game-changer for national defense, industry leadership, and managers at all levels—from major CEOs to convenience store supervisors. With properly constructed queries, AI can deliver exceptionally high-quality data to support decision-making across fields such as manufacturing, mining, automotive, medical, educational, and military domains, among others.

This guide introduces a vital and emerging industry role: the AI Query Engineer. It is designed to provide entry-level familiarity for those new to or transitioning into this field. Readers will gain a foundational understanding of the terminology, logic, and procedures that define this critical position.

Thank you.

Dayle I. Fish

Introduction

AI Query Engineer (Also Referred to as Prompt Engineer)

The vast depth and constant expansion of AI databases create exciting

opportunities for new roles. A "Querier" or AI Query Specialist will be a

valuable job in the future. These professionals would focus on crafting precisely,

creative, and insightful prompts or Queries to maximize the potential of AI systems for a

variety of purposes, such as:

1. Research and Analysis: Formulating complex queries to extract insights

from massive datasets.

2. Creative Content Generation: Designing prompts for storytelling, design,

or brainstorming.

3. Business Problem Solving: Tailoring AI to solve specific challenges or

improve operations.

4. Education and Training: Helping students or workers learn how to use AI

effectively.

5. Customization: Personalizing AI systems for individual or organizational

needs.

Given the rapid evolution of AI, developing the skill to think critically and

Creatively about how to ask is becoming just as important as knowing the answer.

It's a fascinating prospect that underscores the evolving relationship between

humans and technology. If you may be interested in exploring this further or perhaps inspiring others, then please read and study the contents of this AI Query Engineering Guide to gather what Query (or Prompt) Engineering involves.

Interact with your AI system on your computing device as you read through this manual. You will soon be aware that this field may in fact be for you. Good Luck!

Welcome to the AI Query Engineering Guide. This book serves as your foundational resource for understanding and entering one of the most promising and necessary roles in the age of Artificial Intelligence—the AI Query Engineer.

As AI systems continue to evolve and integrate into industries of every kind, a new kind of technical skillset is emerging—one rooted not in coding alone, but in the art and science of crafting queries that retrieve, refine, and apply information at scale. The AI Query Engineer is the person who bridges human intention with machine intelligence through strategic, structured, and sometimes conversational queries.

This Guide has been designed to help new learners, transitioning professionals, and aspiring technologists gain a practical introduction to this role. You'll find real-world terminology, conceptual frameworks, sample queries, and a wide range of structured lesson plans designed to prepare you for practical work in the field.

While this guide is designed with the expectation that a Subject Matter Expert (SME) may lead instruction using the provided lesson plans, readers are also encouraged to independently explore each lesson's Objectives using their AI connection when SME guidance is not available.

To get the most from this guide, we strongly encourage you to interact with AI directly—whether through a mobile device, tablet, or desktop interface. Your learning will grow as you apply each concept in real time, querying AI systems to test, explore, and refine your understanding.

As you work through the chapters and lesson plans, think of yourself as both a student and a practitioner. The exercises and examples are built to mirror the evolving workflows of AI-enhanced industries—from data analysis and natural language processing to decision support and system optimization.

By the end of this guide, you will have built a strong foundation for advancing your skills in AI Query Engineering—and you'll understand how to grow that skillset over time in step with AI itself.

Let's begin.

Preface

I served in the U.S. Navy and retired after more than 23 years of active duty, working in Naval Command and Control Operations around the world—both aboard ships and on command staffs. I rose to the rank of Master Chief Petty Officer and served as Director of Advanced Operations Specialist Training at Dam Neck, Virginia. It was during my time in Vietnam waters, aboard an NTDS (Naval Tactical Data System) cruiser, that I first encountered what we would come to call Digital Warfare.

Following my military service, I continued in the defense sector as a government contractor, performing similar duties at a higher level. I eventually transitioned into software testing, serving for ten years as a Software Test Manager with Northrop Grumman Mission Systems. It was there that we helped develop the renowned Global Command and Control System (GCCS)—a primary decision-support tool for the U.S. military. In the early 2000's, we developed a software for military Co Commander that would allow his staff to "Query" in transit ships and aircraft to determine on board cargo and personnel status. This was my first experience with the title Query but my mind gave the action of what will be accomplished with AI will be as important.

Throughout my entire career, my mission has been singular: to ensure that command decision-makers have access to the most accurate and timely digital data available—often to make life-or-death decisions in real time.

Now, in my 70s, I've approached the emergence of Artificial Intelligence with a profoundly serious interest. This AI technology represents a turning point not only for national defense and industry leadership, but also for managers at every level—from CEOs of major corporations to supervisors of convenience stores. With properly constructed queries, AI can deliver exceptionally high-quality data to support decision-making across fields such as manufacturing, mining, automotive, medical, educational, and military domains, among others.

This Guide introduces a vital and emerging industry role: the AI Query Engineer. It has been created to provide an entry-level familiarity for those new to or transitioning into this field. Readers hopefully will gain a foundational understanding of the terminology, logic, and procedures that define this prominent position.

Thank you.

D.Fish

Chapter 1 Introduction

The field of AI Query Engineering is rapidly evolving, bridging the gap between human interaction and AI-powered data retrieval. This chapter introduces the fundamentals of AI Query Engineering, its importance, and how professionals can leverage AI to optimize data queries effectively.

Section 1: What is AI Query Engineering?

Definition and Scope

AI Query Engineering refers to the structured approach to designing, refining, and optimizing queries for AI-driven systems. This discipline ensures accurate, efficient, and meaningful responses from AI by employing techniques in natural language processing (NLP), database management, and middleware optimization.

Why AI Query Engineering Matters

Enables efficient AI-driven search and data retrieval.

Reduces query processing times through optimized algorithms.

Enhances user interaction with AI systems, improving results accuracy. Ensures middleware compatibility for seamless integration between AI models and databases.

Key Components of AI Query Engineering

Natural Language Query Processing – Understanding and interpreting human-like queries.

Middleware Integration – Optimizing AI-to-database communication.

Query Refinement and Optimization – Structuring queries for efficiency.

Real-Time Query Execution – Leveraging speed layers and edge computing.

Section 2: The Role of AI Query Engineers

Core Responsibilities

AI Query Engineers play a crucial role in enhancing AI's ability to process and respond to queries. Their responsibilities include:

Developing AI-Optimized Query Structures – Designing queries that AI can process efficiently.

Implementing Middleware Solutions – Ensuring smooth interaction between AI, databases, and APIs.

Refining Query Responses – Iteratively improving query logic to enhance AI accuracy.

Monitoring AI Query Performance – Using analytics to assess query efficiency.

Collaborating with AI Developers – Aligning AI query logic with broader AI training objectives.

Skills Required for Senior Level Query Engineers include:

Proficiency in Query Languages (SQL, JSON, GraphQL, API query structures).

Understanding of AI and NLP Models (Transformer models like BERT, GPT).

Middleware and API Optimization (Using RESTful APIs, GraphQL, WebSockets).

Data Structure & Indexing Knowledge (Efficient query execution).

Problem-Solving and Analytical Thinking (Troubleshooting AI query performance).

Section 3: Evolution of AI Query Engineering

Early Days: Manual Query Optimization

Historically, query optimization relied on manual tuning within relational databases (SQL) and static query structures. Engineers had to define rigid parameters for data retrieval, which was time-consuming and lacked adaptability.

Modern AI-Driven Query Processing

With advancements in AI and machine learning, query engineering has evolved into a dynamic field where AI models assist in refining and executing queries in real time. Key innovations include:

Natural Language Querying (NLQ) – Allowing users to interact with AI without structured syntax.

Predictive Query Optimization – AI anticipating query intent and adjusting parameters.

Neural Network-Driven Query Expansion – Using deep learning to refine ambiguous queries.

Edge Computing & Middleware Acceleration – Speeding up query response times in AI-powered applications.

The Future of AI Query Engineering

The next evolution of AI Query Engineering will include:

Integration with Quantum Computing – Redefining query execution speed and complexity.

Autonomous Query Agents – AI systems autonomously refining and executing queries.

Contextual Awareness in Queries – AI understanding user context dynamically.

Section 4: Practical Exercise – AI Query Structuring

Objective:

Understand how AI processes diverse types of queries and optimize them for efficiency.

Steps:

Formulate Natural Language Queries – Write example queries in human language.

Convert to AI-Compatible Query Structures – Translate them into SQL, API requests, or JSON-based formats.

Assess Query Execution – Run the queries through an AI model or database system.

Optimize for Speed & Accuracy – Adjust query parameters and assess improvements.

Assessment Criteria:

Ability to structure queries that AI systems can efficiently interpret.

Improved query execution speed and response accuracy.

Successful conversion of unstructured queries into structured formats.

Summary

This chapter introduced AI Query Engineering, covering its scope, significance, and core responsibilities. We explored how query engineering has evolved from manual optimization to AI-driven processes and outlined future trends in the field.

The next chapter, Core Competencies and Query Engineering Role, will explore the essential skills, career path, and industry applications of an AI Query Engineer.

Next Chapter Preview: Core Competencies and Query Engineering Role:

In the next chapter, we will dive deeper into the key skills required for AI Query Engineers, examining industry applications and best practices for building a successful career in the field.

Chapter 2: Core Competencies of the AI Query Engineer

In the dynamic and evolving world of AI, the AI Query Engineer must possess a unique blend of skills that go beyond basic prompting. These Core Competencies form the foundation of this role and are required for effective collaboration with AI systems, particularly in complex enterprise environments.

1. Understanding Query Construction:

AI Query Engineers must know how to structure questions and tasks clearly and effectively. This includes both natural language and structured query formats. Mastery here enables precise data extraction, transformation, and interpretation from AI systems.

2. Data Format Fluency:

Engineers must work fluently with structured formats like JSON, XML, CSV, and unstructured data. Understanding the syntactic and semantic structure of these formats allows for cleaner integration with AI tools, especially when querying APIs or analyzing datasets.

3. Middleware Integration:

One of the most powerful levers for query optimization, middleware connects front-end interfaces with back-end data systems. A query engineer must know how to utilize and, in some cases, shape middleware to surface the right data efficiently. Mastery includes awareness of GUI elements, API hooks, and speed layer workflows.

:

4. Tools of the trade: Include language models, code interpreters, APIs, visual dashboards, no-code/low-code query platforms, and sometimes scripting environments. A core competency is knowing what tools to use, when, and how to adapt your query strategies across interfaces.

5. Security and Ethics:

A strong AI Query Engineer never bypasses safety. Secure handling of queries and data is essential—especially when personal or sensitive information is involved. Competency in this area includes anonymization techniques, limiting data exposure, understanding system permissions, and staying aware of ethical implications.

6. Feedback Analysis:

Engineers must be capable of evaluating the responses returned by AI. This includes identifying hallucinations, logical fallacies, data gaps, or format issues and refining future queries to improve response quality. It's iterative and often layered.

7. Real-Time Thinking and Iteration:

Many real-world queries require thinking on your feet. You must adapt quickly, iterate on-the-fly, and be comfortable testing your assumptions in real time. This is especially vital when querying complex datasets or multi-turn AI systems.

8. Collaboration with AI:

Beyond tooling, this role involves forming a human-machine partnership. AI Query Engineers learn how to 'think with the machine'—a synergy that enhances productivity, insight generation, and discovery across domains.

9. Communicating Results:

Whether visual, tabular, or narrative, engineers must know how to turn query outputs into actionable insights. This involves storytelling with data and ensuring the results match the needs of stakeholders.

10. Staying Current:

The field is evolving rapidly. Continuous learning, curiosity, and experimentation are not just nice-to-haves—they're survival skills. From new LLM capabilities to evolving API standards, staying current is a core part of the job.

Each competency above will be reinforced throughout this guide in both technical tutorials and real-world case studies. The AI Query Engineer is not just a prompt crafter, they are the bridge between human need and machine capability.

Chapter 3: Middleware as the Core Enabler

Chapter 3: Middleware as the Core Enabler

Middleware serves as the backbone of AI Query Engineering by acting as a bridge between the user interface and the underlying data and systems. It enables rapid, reliable, and organized data transfer, query routing, and response formatting.

Section 1: What is Middleware?

Middleware refers to software that connects different applications, services, and data sources. It handles communication, data management, and task automation. For the AI Query Engineer, middleware provides the platform that translates natural language queries into structured actions.

Section 2: Functions of Middleware in Query Engineering

- Query parsing and routing

- API management and aggregation

- Format conversion (e.g., JSON to structured tables)

- GUI development for query entry

- Access control and permissions

- Real-time monitoring and logging

Section 3: The Speed Layer

Middleware enables the "speed layer," a concept representing the system's ability to handle real-time, low-latency queries and responses. This is essential when milliseconds matter—such as in dashboard updates, inventory checks, or mobile commands. It integrates with real-time data sources, caches, and microservices to ensure immediate access.

Section 4: Security and Monitoring (Middleware Extension)

Security features embedded in middleware allow for centralized authentication, encryption of queries and results, rate-limiting, and role-based access. Monitoring tools enable traceability of query flow, detection of anomalies, and performance logging—critical for any organization relying on secure AI interaction.

Section 5: Middleware GUI and Speed Layer Examples

Modern middleware often includes graphical interfaces for entering queries. These GUIs, built on industry APIs, allow natural language input and offer real-time data sorting, filtering, and visualization. Middleware also offers templated query forms that convert GUI inputs into structured requests.

Section 6: Future Direction

As middleware evolves, AI Query Engineers will be expected to understand more about service orchestration, auto-scaling, and cross-system data virtualization. They must stay ahead of middleware trends and leverage its increasing role in automating and securing the query.

Chapter 4: Advanced Middleware Techniques

This chapter prepares readers for the advanced middleware applications covered in Chapter 4 and real-world examples found in Addendum A.

This chapter explores advanced strategies and tools that empower AI Query Engineers to harness middleware for scalable, secure, and high-performance querying. It extends the concepts introduced in Chapter 3 by diving deeper into optimization, resilience, and the interface between middleware and emerging AI tools.

Section 1: Best Practices Speed Layer Enhancement

AI Query Engineers must work closely with middleware developers to fine-tune the Speed Layer for maximum efficiency. This includes implementing:

- Streamlined API endpoints for low-latency responses

- Intelligent query routing using decision trees or rulesets

- Temporary memory stores for high-frequency data

- Scheduled cache refreshing to balance performance and freshness

Section 2: Middleware as the Backbone

Middleware is the AI Query Engineer's most reliable tool. It:

- Provides seamless, low-latency communication between frontend and backend systems

- Organizes query results into clean data visualizations

- Manages data flow and ensures that queries are trackable and secure

- Generates query logs to monitor misuse or optimization opportunities

Section 3: Interoperability

Interoperability allows multiple systems to interact through middleware, regardless of vendor, format, or architecture. An AI Query Engineer must:

- Work with APIs and translation layers

- Understand cross-platform authorization mechanisms

- Design workflows that connect databases, cloud systems, and AI models in real-time

Section 4: Lightweight Introduction to ML Product Access Tools

Middleware is now integrating lightweight ML tools to offer predictive insights directly to the AI Query Engineer. This includes:

- Sentiment scoring APIs

- Image classification endpoints

- Pretrained recommendation engines

- Semantic search interfaces

These tools allow queries to do more than retrieve—they now anticipate and suggest. Middleware packages these ML tools and exposes them through endpoints or visual forms.

Section 5: Entry-Level Middleware Query Exercise

To help future AI Query Engineers build confidence, students should experiment with mock interfaces that simulate query construction and real-time feedback. A starter scenario might include:

- A GUI interface connected to a middleware simulator

- Query like: "What were the top 3 error codes returned from API endpoints last week?"

- The middleware simulator parses the question, identifies the relevant dataset, and simulates a response in JSON

This exercise fosters understanding of query structure, routing logic, and the real-world impact of query quality.

Chapter Summary:

This chapter has provided a hands-on view of advanced middleware mechanics. As middleware matures, AI Query Engineers must move beyond consumption to influence—understanding its flows, optimizing its speed, and evaluating its machine-learning-enhanced outputs. Middleware isn't a black box, it's a powerful, inspectable ally.

Preview of Chapter 5:

The next chapter transitions to the broader support ecosystem for the AI Query Engineer, including tools, resources, and the rise of edge computing. You'll learn how edge devices and local processing support real-time query needs, and how AI Query Engineers can integrate visualization tools, security monitors, and sandbox environments to test, refine, and deliver their solutions with speed and confidence.

Additional Middleware Practice Queries (4 Examples):

1. **Query for Latency Monitoring**

"Retrieve the average response time for all active middleware endpoints over the past 12 hours."

2. **Cross-System Query Routing**

"Track which external APIs were accessed through the middleware in the last 3 days, and group them by frequency."

3. **Security Layer Verification**

"List all user roles that triggered security exceptions when querying through the middleware interface this week."

4. **Semantic Search Middleware Query**

"Using semantic search integration, summarize the top 3 user-submitted queries that were resolved using predictive completion."

These exercises deepen your ability to think across system layers, security policies, and intelligent features enabled by middleware.

Chapter 5: Tools, Resources, and Edge Computing

This Chapter shifts the focus from core query methods to the broader ecosystem that supports AI Query Engineers in the field. This includes a look at the tools, data visualization environments, edge computing platforms, and sandbox environments that allow engineers to iterate, test, and deliver solutions quickly and securely.

Section 1: An Introduction to Edge Computing

Edge computing refers to processing data close to where it's generated, rather than sending it to a centralized data center. For AI Query Engineers, this means queries that:

- Interact with edge devices like IoT sensors, mobile units, or localized servers

- Require immediate data feedback (e.g. factory alerts or live logistics)

- Must operate offline or with minimal latency

Edge computing enables:

- On-device AI querying with preloaded models

- Local database caching for repeated query calls

- Reduced reliance on cloud-only infrastructure

Section 2: Tools that Empower the AI Query Engineer

AI Query Engineers often use the following categories of tools:

- **Low-code GUI query builders**: These allow drag-and-drop workflows tied to natural language input.

- **API test clients**: Tools like Postman or Insomnia help simulate requests and analyze responses.

- **AI-enabled IDEs**: Integrations with language models assist in building and refining code-based queries.

- **Real-time data monitors**: Tools that track response times, query failures, and usage metrics.

Additionally, robust middleware often includes its own toolkit that allows:

- Logging and tracing queries

- Rebuilding query templates

- Testing APIs and security behavior

- Running simulations against sandboxed datasets

Section 3: Sandbox Environments and Query Validation

Sandbox environments control test spaces where AI Query Engineers may experiment without impacting production systems. Features of a good sandbox:

- Mock APIs and simulated delays

- Test datasets with varying edge cases

- Alert systems for identifying problematic queries

- Embedded monitoring tools to track query costs or computer load

Section 4: Visualization Resources

Once a query is successful, it often needs to be communicated visually. Query Engineers can export data into:

- Interactive dashboards (e.g., Tableau, Power BI)

- Charting libraries (e.g., D3.js, Chart.js)

- PDF or print reports with data annotations

Some middleware platforms include built-in visualization options tied to query output.

Chapter 5 Summary:

This chapter introduced the practical ecosystem tools and environments that AI Query Engineers use daily. From edge computing to sandbox testing, these tools allow for real-time experimentation, validation, and results presentation. They also help query engineers work closer to where data lives—whether on the cloud, on-device, or in a secure testbed.

Preview of Chapter 6:

In Chapter 6, you'll explore a series of real-world case studies that illustrate how AI Query Engineers operate in industries such as finance, logistics, and healthcare. These examples will highlight how core competencies, middleware, and query construction skills come together in high-impact scenarios.

Chapter 6: Case Studies in Query Engineering

This chapter presents real-world case studies demonstrating the role of an AI Query Engineer in optimizing, troubleshooting, and improving query-based workflows. By analyzing these examples, readers will gain insight into best practices, challenges, and the methodologies that define a successful AI Query Engineer's approach.

Case Study 1: Optimizing Middleware Query Performance

Scenario: A financial services company struggled with slow query response times, impacting real-time customer transactions.

Problem:

- Middleware queries interacting with multiple databases resulted in excessive latency due to redundant queries and inefficient indexing.

Solution:

- Implemented caching mechanisms for frequently accessed data.

- Rewrote queries to leverage optimized indexing strategies.

- Reduced the number of redundant API calls by structuring a more efficient query pipeline.

Outcome:

- 40% improvement in query response time.

- Reduced computational load on the database by 30%.

- Enhanced customer experience with real-time transaction processing.

Case Study 2: Enhancing AI-Powered Search for E-Commerce

Scenario: An e-commerce company implemented an AI-driven product search feature but faced inaccurate and slow search results.

Problem:

- Poor query structuring led to irrelevant search results.

- The middleware was not efficiently utilizing vector embeddings and keyword matching.

Solution:

- Introduced a hybrid search approach combining keyword-based search with semantic search using embeddings.

- Fine-tuned AI model parameters to improve result ranking and relevance.

- Optimized middleware query execution to leverage indexed precomputed embeddings.

Outcome:

- Increased search result relevance by 50%.

- Improved conversion rates due to better product recommendations.

- Enhanced system efficiency with preprocessed embeddings reducing query overhead.

Case Study 3: Automating Query Optimization in Healthcare Analytics

Scenario: A healthcare provider faced performance bottlenecks in

processing large-scale patient data queries.

Problem:

- Complex queries were being executed inefficiently, leading to extended processing times.

- Lack of query optimization techniques such as indexing and partitioning.

Solution:

- Introduced AI-driven query optimization to analyze query patterns and suggest performance improvements.

- Applied data partitioning to improve indexing efficiency.

- Implemented an intelligent caching mechanism for frequently requested datasets.

Outcome:

- 60% reduction in query execution time.

- Improved data retrieval efficiency, allowing real-time patient data insights.

- Enhanced compliance with healthcare regulations by ensuring faster data access.

Case Study 4: Scaling AI Query Systems for a Global Logistics Firm

Scenario: A logistics company needed to scale its AI-driven shipment tracking system as demand increased.

Problem:

- Middleware queries overloaded the database due to inefficient query batching.

- API rate limits were frequently exceeded, causing disruptions in tracking updates.

Solution:

- Designed an intelligent query batching mechanism to consolidate similar queries.

- Implemented a middleware-based query prioritization system.

- Used edge computing to preprocess for tracking data closer to the source.

Outcome:

- Increased system scalability to handle 5x more queries.

- Reduced API overuse and improved real-time shipment tracking.

- Minimized server costs by 35% through more efficient data handling.

Summary

Through these case studies, we have seen how AI Query Engineers diagnose and resolve challenges related to query efficiency, middleware performance, AI-powered search, and system scalability. By applying these lessons, Query Engineers can create optimized, high-performance AI query systems tailored to diverse industry needs.

Next Chapter Preview

In Chapter 7: AI Query Fundamentals, This chapter introduces fundamental query types

Chapter 7: AI Query Fundamentals

This chapter introduces the fundamental query types and structures that AI Query Engineers must master to perform effectively in both training and real-world environments. Building strong, clean queries is essential, and this chapter emphasizes the importance of query clarity, specificity, verbosity when appropriate, and structured logic. It includes examples, logic explanations, and commentary to help engineers understand when and why certain styles are best applied.

◆ Types of Natural Language Queries and Their Use Cases

1. Specific & Direct Query
"Show me all error logs from server cluster B between 2:00 a.m. and 6:00 a.m. yesterday."
→ Used when precision and scope are tightly defined.

2. Verbose Query for Exhaustive Results
"List all transactions over $10,000 that were flagged for manual review, include customer names, transaction dates, and reasons for flagging."
→ Useful in audit trails or investigations.

3. Procedural Query
"What steps must be taken to restart the API gateway service without affecting current user sessions?"
→ Common in ops support and knowledge base retrieval.

4. Sentiment Analysis Request
"Summarize positive user comments about the new 'dark mode' feature since its release."
→ Used for product feedback loops, often coupled with semantic parsing.

5. Comparative Query
"Compare system performance metrics before and after patch v2.14 deployment."
→ Valuable in regression analysis or benchmarking scenarios.

6. Diagnostic Query
"Identify which middleware nodes had more than three dropped requests in the last hour."
→ Useful for alerting and health checks.

7. Predictive Pattern Request
"Based on past data, which customers are likely to churn within the next month?"
→ Often sent to or through ML models.

8. Descriptive Visualization Query
"Create a time series graph of bandwidth consumption per user group for the past 30 days."
→ Typically fed into visualization middleware.

9. Summarization Query
"Summarize all updates from the last three sprint reports into a single bullet-point list."
→ Great for condensing data across sources.

10. Batch Query for Industrial Use

"For each 7nm chip batch produced in February, list average defect rates, downtime hours, and operator IDs."

→ Used in manufacturing and industrial telemetry analysis.

11. Layered Conditional Query

"If more than five security events occurred at any site in the last 12 hours, list the top three by severity."

→ Advanced logic pattern useful in conditional automation.

12. Time-Bound Summation Query

"Give total inbound API requests per hour for the past 48 hours."

→ Quick analytics dashboard-style request.

13. Drill Down Query

"From the top five performing sales regions this quarter, show the customer segments contributing most to revenue."

→ Explores layered data relationships.

14. Escalation Trigger Query

"Alert me if any node in Region A fails to respond twice in under 10 minutes."

→ Sets the basis for real-time monitoring workflows.

15. Enrichment Query

"Enrich customer data with the latest firmographic details from public business registries."

→ Often tied to external API ingestion.

◆ Logic Behind Query Creation

Each natural language query should:

- Target a clear objective (retrieve, summarize, compare, diagnose, visualize)
- Identify temporal constraints where relevant
- Specify output structure or fields, if known
- Align to available middleware or API capacity
- Use vocabulary appropriate to the user GUI or speed layer framework

By training on these varied patterns, the AI Query Engineer gains flexibility and precision. Each query form is a tool in a growing toolkit, selected based on situation, response latency, and data structure involved.

✅ **Case Study Example 1**: Sentiment Analysis
Query: "Summarize positive user comments about the new 'dark mode' feature since its release."

- Goal: Feedback aggregation for UI improvement.
- Target: Sentiment parser linked to product review API.
- Middleware Role: Segmenting, classifying, summarizing content.
- Output: Bullet list of representative positive statements and frequency.

✅ **Case Study Example 2**: Semiconductor Manufacturing
Query: "For each 7nm chip batch produced in February, list average defect rates, downtime hours, and operator IDs."

- Goal: Batch quality analysis.
- Target: Manufacturing database with metadata logs.
- Middleware Role: Aggregate, filter by timestamp, join relational tables.
- Output: Structured table for engineering review.

By the end of this chapter, engineers should be able to:

- Formulate 10+ distinct query types
- Understand how verbosity, precision, and logic shape query outcomes
- Match query structure to appropriate middleware responses
- Prepare queries suitable for visual dashboards, summaries, or alerting systems

Lesson Plan: Constructing Natural Language Batch Queries (NLM Batch Queries)

Topic:

Building and Structuring Effective NLM Batch Queries for Scalable AI Use

Objectives:

By the end of this lesson, participants will be able to:

1. Understand the principles of batch querying in AI contexts.

2. Design modular, scalable, and clear natural language batch queries.

3. Construct multi-step, logic-driven batch queries for real-world scenarios.

4. Practice hands-on construction of batch queries across domains.

Materials:

- Whiteboard or digital equivalent

- LLM access (e.g., ChatGPT or API)

- Sample datasets or business tasks

- Query templates

- Note-taking tools

1. Introduction to NLM Batch Queries (10 minutes)

Concept: Batch queries are collections of well-structured natural language inputs designed to be submitted sequentially or simultaneously to an LLM, either for automation, analysis, or multi-domain problem solving.

Use Case Examples:

- A healthcare team querying for treatment summaries across 500 conditions

- A manufacturing plant querying for optimal production settings across 30 machine types

- An HR department generating tailored job descriptions for 20 open roles

2. Core Concepts of Batch Queries (15 minutes)

Key Features:

- Scalability

- Reusability

- Clarity

- Automation-ready

Illustration:

Instead of:

> "Summarize diabetes care."

Use:

> "Using plain language suitable for patients, summarize standard care steps for Type 2 Diabetes including medication, diet, and exercise."

Then replicate structure:

> "Using plain language suitable for patients, summarize standard care steps for Hypertension..."

3. Designing Effective Batch Queries (25 minutes)

• Clarity: Use specific, jargon-reduced, unambiguous language

Example:

> Poor: "What do I do about safety?"

> Better: "List 5 OSHA-mandated daily safety checks for forklift operation in a warehouse."

• Consistency: Maintain format across queries

Example:

- "Summarize the top 3 causes of..."

- "Summarize the top 3 risks of..."

- "Summarize the top 3 solutions to..."

• Modularity: Break complex questions into structured sub-queries

Example:

Instead of:

> "How can we increase productivity across all departments?"

Break into:

1. "What are three productivity KPIs for the logistics department?"

2. "What factors most affect productivity in logistics?"

3. "Suggest three improvements based on those factors."

Practice Activity:

Participants draft three consistent batch queries across a single topic:

Example Domain: Environmental Reporting

- "List top 5 pollutants tracked by EPA in 2024."

- "Summarize each pollutant's primary industrial source."

- "Suggest mitigation strategies for each pollutant."

4. Hands-On Exercise: Constructing Batch Queries (30 minutes)

Goal: Develop a 5-query batch addressing a scenario of the participant's choosing (e.g., training, sales, operations, medical).

Instructions:

Participants choose a domain and then construct 5 queries using the batch structure principles. They must:

1. Select a scenario (e.g., onboarding new employees)

2. Draft modular queries (e.g., one per training topic)

3. Keep structure consistent

4. Review each for clarity, modularity, and reuse

Example Scenario: New Employee Training

- "What are the 3 most critical policies to include in first-day training?"

- "Provide a 100-word summary of each policy suitable for email."

- "Draft a quiz question for each policy with 3 answer choices."

- "Suggest a visual aid for each policy's explanation."

- "What follow-up materials should be emailed one week later?"

Facilitator Tip: Review queries in pairs and iterate once for clarity improvement.

5. Application & Feedback (10 minutes)

Participants test one of their batch queries live (if access to LLM is available, will work on GPS4, then receive group feedback on structure and clarity. Encourage iteration.

6. Summary and Takeaway (5 minutes)

- Batch queries help scale LLM use with less manual effort

- They depend on good design, structure, and language discipline

- Clear, modular, and consistent formatting improves reliability

- Reusable structures save time and improve accuracy

Assignment (Optional): Convert a personal or team workflow into a 5-part batch query set for use in your workplace or consulting effort.

Chapter 8: An Introduction to Neural Networks

This chapter introduces neural networks as a foundational concept that underpins many of the intelligent systems leveraged by AI Query Engineers. It explains how neural networks are trained, how they interpret queries and data, and how they can be used to improve semantic understanding and inference generation in the context of structured querying environments.

◆ What Is a Neural Network?

A neural network is a set of algorithms modeled loosely after the human brain that is designed to recognize patterns. It interprets sensory data through machine perception, labeling, or clustering of raw input. Neural networks are the backbone of most modern large language models (LLMs), powering capabilities like:

- Semantic search
- Predictive typing
- Natural language understanding
- Intent classification

Neural networks are trained using massive datasets, adjusting internal parameters such as weights and biases across layers to improve prediction accuracy over time.

◆ Key Concepts for Query Engineers

- Weights & Biases: These determine the strength and direction of signals passed between artificial neurons. Engineers don't usually adjust them directly but benefit from understanding how models prioritize input.

- Embeddings: Vectors representing text or data that capture semantic meaning. Similar concepts are mapped close together in high-dimensional space. Query Engineers may leverage these for:
  - Semantic search
  - Clustering user intent
  - Synonym handling

- Hidden Layers: Where the network extracts progressively abstract features. The more layers, the deeper (and often more powerful) the model.

- Activation Functions: Determine whether a neuron "fires" or not. ReLU, sigmoid, and softmax are common.

◆ Practical Applications in Query Engineering

Neural networks support many advanced use cases in AI querying:

- Semantic Search Engines: Interpret user queries based on meaning, not just keywords.
- Autocomplete & Suggestion Systems: Predict likely next inputs using deep learning.
- Middleware Optimization: Neural models can classify or rank middleware responses to streamline outputs.
- Natural Language to SQL or API: Convert NL queries to backend-executable code.

Query Engineers should become familiar with APIs or GUIs that expose these functionalities—especially those offering access to embeddings, relevance scores, and pre-trained inference tools.

✅ Case Study: Query Interpretation Using BERT

Scenario: A user types: "Find contractors who were late on projects but not penalized."

System: A BERT-based model breaks this into intent, conditions, and exclusions.

- Embedding Analysis: Understands "late on projects" and "not penalized" as connected but distinct conditions.
- Query Expansion: Includes synonyms like "delayed" and "no penalty imposed."
- Execution: Converts user intent into structured middleware call filtering two criteria.

Result: Accurate, nuanced response pulled from semi-structured contract data.

◆ Next Steps for Query Engineers

To move forward in using neural networks:
- Explore platforms offering embedding visualizations (like OpenAI, Cohere, or Hugging Face)
- Test queries in semantic-aware tools
- Learn how to structure verbose queries to increase clarity for underlying models

While AI Query Engineers don't need to build neural networks, they do need to understand how they interpret language and deliver outputs—and how that can shape their own queries for maximum effect.

By understanding neural networks, engineers strengthen their ability to interact with modern AI systems at a high level—whether guiding a middleware interface, analyzing feedback loops, or querying intelligent endpoints across the enterprise.

Addendum A: Lesson Plans for AI Query Engineers

It was anticipated that these lessons plans would be used by AI Query Engineering Subject Matter Experts.

Failing their availability, Readers are encouraged to use their computing device to Query the individual Objectives, for a full description.

Lesson Plan: Advanced Middleware Techniques

**Topic: ** Advanced Middleware Techniques

Objectives:

- - Understand how middleware functions as a speed layer
- - Demonstrate the use of middleware APIs for query routing
- - Identify how GUI-based query systems rely on middleware

Materials:

- - Middleware architecture diagrams
- - Sample GUI querying tool
- - Case study examples

Introduction: Begin with a real-time query simulation that fails due to middleware absence. Discuss the result and contrast with middleware-enabled systems.

Presentation: Explain middleware layers, present real-world examples, and demonstrate API-driven middleware. Walk through how queries are processed in the speed layer.

Summary: Students should explain the role of middleware in query processing and demonstrate a middleware-supported query via GUI or script.

Lesson Plan 1: Middleware Security and Monitoring

Topic: Middleware Security and Monitoring

Objectives:

- - Recognize vulnerabilities in middleware systems
- - Explain key principles of secure query transmission
- - Demonstrate logging and monitoring tools

Materials:

- - Sample logs
- - Security flowcharts
- - Middleware monitoring dashboard access

Introduction: Present a simulated middleware breach scenario and ask students to identify the security gap.

Presentation: Walk through secure API practices, explain token authentication, logging layers, and demonstrate real-time monitoring on a dashboard.

Summary: Students should be able to explain middleware security basics and identify what monitoring metrics are essential.

Lesson Plan 2: Case Studies in Query Engineering

Topic: Case Studies in Query Engineering

Objectives:

- - Analyze real-world query scenarios
- - Evaluate query strategy effectiveness
- - Design improved queries for specific use case **Materials:**
- - Printed case studies
- - Query templates
- - Mock dashboard interface

Introduction: Review a flawed query result and ask students how it could have been improved.

Presentation: Dissect two real case studies, show the impact of revised queries, and walk through a live improvement.

Summary: Students should describe the learning from each case study and demonstrate their own refined queries.

Lesson Plan: Tools and Resources: Edge Computing and Query Speed

Topic: Tools and Resources: Edge Computing and Query Speed

Objectives:

- - Understand the architecture of edge computing in AI systems
- - Use queries to interact with edge-deployed nodes
- - Recognize the role of edge in low-latency systems

Materials:

- - Edge gateway diagrams
- - IoT simulation tools
- - Query GUI connected to simulated edge environment

Introduction: Pose a problem of delayed data from cloud-only systems. Ask how edge could help.

Presentation: Introduce edge-node concepts, show middleware role, and execute sample queries on edge-connected datasets.

Summary: Students explain how edge computing improves performance and write a sample edge query.

Topic: Building Middleware Speed Layers

Objectives:

- - Map the components of a speed layer
- - Identify query flow from user to result
- - Explore API integration within middleware

Materials:

- - Speed layer framework poster
- - Sample code for middleware routing
- - API documentation

Introduction: Introduce a timeline of system response with and without a speed layer.

Presentation: Explain how queries are accelerated, walk through sample request-response flow, and explore middleware orchestration.

In the context of the Lamda Architecture or similar data processing systems, the Speed Layer accelerates queries through several key mechanisms:

In-Memory Processing, Incremental Computation, Denormalized Views, Indexing Strategies, Real-Time Data Structures, Distributed Processing, Query Optimization, and Caching.

Summary: Students map a query from front end to backend and describe where speed improvements occur.

Lesson Plan: Middleware in Action: Enabling a Query GUI

Topic: Middleware in Action: Enabling a Query GUI

Objectives:

- - Show how middleware powers user-friendly query interfaces
- - Demonstrate API call construction from GUI input
- - Understand formatting of backend responses

Materials:

- - Sample GUI interfaces
- - Code snippets for middleware calls
- - Middleware logs

Introduction: Ask students to input a natural language query and guess what system calls are being made.

Presentation: Display the conversion path from GUI to middleware to API and back. Show logs and resulting data structures.

Summary: Students trace a GUI-driven query through middleware and explain each transformation.

Addendum B: Core Competency Expansions

Middleware as the Speed Layer
Middleware acts as the 'speed layer' in AI Query Engineering by handling the fast routing, processing, and response generation between user interfaces and back-end data systems. It provides the architecture necessary to translate natural language queries into API calls, aggregate results, apply logic filters, and display output dynamically within milliseconds. Middleware also enables real-time monitoring, filtering, and even reformatting of results to match specific user roles or dashboards. Understanding its role as the connective tissue across all layers of the AI stack is essential to mastering advanced query systems.

Interoperability in Query Systems
Interoperability ensures that queries can travel seamlessly between diverse systems, data formats, and platforms. In query engineering, it means crafting queries that can operate through different middleware gateways, connect across enterprise APIs, and return standardized results. It also involves understanding data structure mapping, transformation layers, and the vocabulary of shared endpoints.

Edge Computing and the Role of the Query Engineer
Edge computing reshapes the scope of query engineering by pushing computation closer to the data source. This empowers Query Engineers to write localized queries that retrieve or act upon data at the edge node level—improving latency, uptime, and bandwidth usage. It also requires

understanding of which APIs, models, and alerting systems live at the edge and how to work within decentralized system designs.

Query Procedures for Mobile Command Units

In tactical or field-based environments like mobile command units, AI Query Engineers must craft robust, reliable queries for low-connectivity zones. These procedures involve local caching, offline inference, and time-delayed logging. Middleware must also account for sudden reconnection events, and queries should be optimized for both edge processing and post-reintegration analysis.

Drill Down and Around: Chain of Thought (CoT) Querying

Query Engineers often need to begin with a top-level summary and then perform 'drill down and around' procedures—exploring subcategories, alternate perspectives, and relationships between data points. This mental framework reinforces strategic query thinking, enabling engineers to break a problem into layers, design stepwise follow-up queries, and synthesize results from multiple angles.

Addendum C: Chapters Exam   C: Exams – Tests 1 May Be Open Book Test, but Please Complete

Test 1: Chapters 1–3 (True/False)

1. The title 'AI Query Engineer' is more professional than 'Prompt Engineer'. (True/False)

2. Chapter 1 explains how to install Python for AI development. (True/False)

3. A core role of the AI Query Engineer is to build effective queries for LLMs. (True/False)

4. The AI Query Engineer's career path typically begins as a Senior Engineer. (True/False)

5. Query Engineers must understand business logic as well as technical systems. (True/False)

6. Middleware is only used in data storage, not in query management. (True/False)

7. Security monitoring is an optional feature of middleware. (True/False)

8. Chapter 3 introduces the role of middleware in speeding up AI queries. (True/False)

9. Query Engineers do not need to worry about data formats. (True/False)

10. Middleware API's allow access to external databases and services. (True/False)

11. The term 'Speed Layer' refers to middleware's rapid data access capability. (True/False)

12. Chapter 2 outlines the daily workflow of a Query Engineer. (True/False)

13. Query Engineers never work with security protocols. (True/False)

14. Middleware can format data for display in GUIs. (True/False)

15. A Query Engineer should avoid working with natural language queries. (True/False)

16. Query Engineers are expected to understand system interoperability. (True/False)

17. Middleware enhances both security and speed in AI systems. (True/False)

18. Acronyms and terminology are not discussed until Chapter 8. (True/False)

19. Queries can be optimized by understanding how middleware operates. (True/False)

20. Monitoring systems detect unauthorized access attempts. (True/False)

21. APIs in middleware are not accessible to Query Engineers. (True/False)

22. Chapter 1 introduces the main steam cycle as an analogy. (True/False)

23. The AI Query Guide recommends hands-on learning via AI tools. (True/False)

24. Chapter 2 introduces the Query Engineer's expected tools. (True/False)

25. Middleware systems are outside the scope of this guide. (True/False)

Answer Key: Test 1

1. True

2. False

3. True

4. False

5. True

6. False

7. False

8. True

9. False

10. True

11. True

12. True

13. False

14. True

15. False

16. True

17. True

18. False

19. True

20. True

21. False

22. True

23. True

24. True

25. False

25-Test 2, Question True/False Exam – Chapters 3–5: Middleware, Speed Layer, and Edge Computing

May Be Open Book Test, but Please Complete

Name: _____   Date: _____

Instructions: Circle T for True or F for False.

1. T / F Middleware acts as the direct user interface in most AI Query systems.

2. T / F The Speed Layer is responsible for storing long-term historical data.

3. T / F Middleware APIs allow for data exchange between front-end interfaces and backend systems.

4. T / F The Speed Layer is designed to deliver rapid responses from real-time data.

5. T / F Middleware can help enforce security policies between systems.

6. T / F Query Engineers typically design and manufacture physical middleware devices.

7. T / F An AI Query GUI can be powered by middleware and connected through APIs.

8. T / F The Speed Layer is optional in real-time AI-driven systems.

9. T / F Middleware helps decouple application logic from data sources.

10. T / F Monitoring and observability tools are irrelevant for middleware operations.

11. T / F APIs are often used to support different formats of incoming data within middleware.

12. T / F Edge Computing focuses on centralizing data processing at headquarters.

13. T / F Edge devices process data close to where it is generated.

14. T / F The Speed Layer is mainly used to store backup data.

15. T / F Middleware provides translation services between incompatible data systems.

16. T / F Edge Computing can reduce latency in AI Query responses.

17. T / F Edge devices should always send raw data back to the cloud for processing.

18. T / F One function of middleware is to log user queries for security auditing.

19. T / F Speed Layer components usually rely on batch-processing workflows.

20. T / F API throttling and rate limits can be managed through middleware layers.

21. T / F Speed Layers are most useful when response time is not important.

22. T / F Middleware simplifies the complexity of integrating multiple systems.

23. T / F Edge Computing is irrelevant for mobile AI deployments.

24. T / F A well-designed middleware layer enables scalable AI services.

25. T / F The Speed Layer's data is often discarded after it serves its immediate purpose.

Answer Key – Test 2

1. F

2. F

3. T

4. T

5. T

6. F

7. T

8. F

9. T

10. F

11. T

12. F

13. T

14. F

15. T

16. T

17. F

18. T

19. F

20. T

21. F

22. T

23. F

24. T

25. T

Test 3, 25-Question True/False Exam – Chapters 6–8: Case Studies, Query

May Be Open **Book Test, but please complete.**

Fundamentals, and Neural Networks

Name: _____   Date: _____

Instructions: Circle T for True or F for False.

1. T / F A case study can be a practical tool for understanding how natural language queries perform in real-world scenarios.

2. T / F The 7nm chip batch query case study focused on agricultural data.

3. T / F AI Query Fundamentals include understanding how to structure queries for precision and clarity.

4. T / F Natural language queries must always be long to be effective.

5. T / F Case studies can show both successful and failed query implementations.

6. T / F Sentiment analysis is used in one case study to evaluate mobile app feedback.

7. T / F Neural networks mimic the human brain's structure using interconnected nodes.

8. T / F Embeddings help neural networks assign meaning to different forms of input.

9. T / F AI Query Engineers never need to understand how weights and biases affect neural models.

10. T / F The BERT case study demonstrates the use of transformers in modern AI models.

11. T / F A well-written NL query should aim for both clarity and specificity.

12. T / F Neural networks are typically used to execute firewall rules in middleware.

13. T / F The fundamentals of querying are not important once a GUI is available.

14. T / F Verbose language in queries can lead to hallucinated results in LLMs.

15. T / F Semantic search can be improved using neural embeddings.

16. T / F Query logic is unrelated to the structure of the underlying data.

17. T / F A Query Engineer should be capable of refining queries based on observed outputs.

18. T / F Neural networks learn by adjusting weights through training cycles.

19. T / F Context and intent are key components of well-structured queries.

20. T / F In the BERT model, all words in a sentence are processed sequentially with no parallelism.

21. T / F Case studies in the guide help reinforce how middleware interacts with queries.

22. T / F A simple T/F test like this cannot be used to assess basic AI knowledge.

23. T / F Neural networks cannot be used for visual data processing.

24. T / F The Query Fundamentals chapter emphasizes critical thinking in prompt design.

25. T / F Embeddings allow LLMs to handle semantically similar inputs more intelligently.

Answer Key – Test 3

1. T

2. F

3. T

4. F

5. T

6. T

7. T

8. T

9. F

10. T

11. T

12. F

13. F

14. T

15. T

16. F

17. T

18. T

19. T

20. F

21. T

22. F

23. F

24. T

25. T

AI Query Engineering Guide Final Exam

May Be Open Book Test, but please complete.

True/False Exam: 50 Questions

1. The title 'AI Query Engineer' was chosen to reflect a more professional and technical role than 'Prompt Engineer.'

2. Middleware is optional for translating natural language queries into structured outputs.

3. Natural language queries can be verbose when the goal is to increase clarity.

4. Edge computing reduces latency by moving processing closer to data sources.

5. The speed layer is primarily concerned with graphical rendering.

6. Query Engineers may use semantic search to return meaning-based results.

7. APIs are irrelevant to AI Query Engineering workflows.

8. GUI tools often depend on middleware to communicate with databases.

9. BERT is a model capable of understanding contextual relationships between words.

10. Diagnostic queries are used to monitor performance and detect system issues.

11. Middleware logs are never used in query optimization.

12. A case study in Chapter 6 showed how improving query phrasing changed the system's outcome.

13. Semantic embeddings help identify related meanings across different terms.

14. Query Engineers should ignore query tone and language for speed.

15. Middleware often includes security layers such as API token validation and monitoring.

16. Batch queries are never used in modern AI systems.

17. Chapter 3 describes middleware as integral to speed layer performance.

18. Natural language to SQL conversion is a role for some AI systems that assist Query Engineers.

19. Visual dashboards often rely on structured outputs from queries.

20. Time-bound queries specify a time frame for data collection or filtering.

21. Edge nodes cannot run ML inference models due to hardware constraints.

22. Enrichment queries involve bringing in new external data to enhance results.

23. The 'drill down and around' method involves exploring data from multiple perspectives.

24. API calls from middleware can include filters, sorts, and joins.

25. Predictive queries always require custom models built from scratch.

26. The Associate, Engineer, Senior Engineer progression was introduced in Chapter 2.

27. Query Engineers must only rely on cloud systems for speed optimization.

28. Synonyms are not useful in semantic-aware queries.

29. Structured thinking is essential for layering query logic.

30. Summarization queries are best used to combine multiple updates or inputs.

31. Visual interfaces do not affect how users formulate queries.

32. Case files are meant to test theoretical concepts only, not real-world queries.

33. Real-time alerting systems can be configured through escalation trigger queries.

34. GUI-generated queries typically pass through a middleware interpreter.

35. Knowledge of GUI structure helps in writing better middleware-compatible queries.

36. Middleware never handles security or logging.

37. Embeddings represent text as numeric vectors in high-dimensional space.

38. Edge computing is irrelevant in healthcare or logistics systems.

39. Engineers should practice different query types including diagnostic and enrichment.

40. Natural language interfaces will likely play a growing role in enterprise systems.

41. The Query Engineering Guide discourages hands-on experimentation.

42. Middleware sometimes reorders or transforms data before display.

43. Large language models can be used to translate natural language into backend queries.

44. JSON is a format often used in API responses and middleware transactions.

45. Summarization queries are only applicable to structured databases.

46. GUI queries can be built around available middleware endpoints.

47. Security features are not part of a Query Engineer's knowledge base.

48. Drill-down queries help explore contributing factors in top-level data.

49. Natural language queries are the same regardless of context or audience.

50. Tangled qubits may one day enhance the speed layer via quantum computing.

Answer Key – Final Exam

1. True

2. False

3. True

4. True

5. False

6. True

7. False

8. True

9. True

10. True

11. False

12. True

13. True

14. False

15. True

16. False

17. True

18. True

19. True

20. True

21. False

22. True

23. True

24. True

25. False

26. True

27. False

28. False

29. True

30. True

31. False

32. False

33. True

34. True

35. True

36. False

37. True

38. False

39. True

40. True

41. False

42. True

43. True

44. True

45. False

46. True

47. False

48. True

49. False

50. True

Bibliography & References

Primary Sources

Goodfellow, I., Bengio, Y., & Courville, A. (2016). Deep Learning. MIT Press.
Covers foundational neural network principles and applications relevant to AI query optimization.

Russell, S., & Norvig, P. (2020). Artificial Intelligence: A Modern Approach (4th ed.). Pearson.
Explores AI methodologies, including query engineering and intelligent middleware applications.

Stonebraker, M., & Çetintemel, U. (2005). "One Size Fits All": An Idea Whose Time Has Come and Gone. Proceedings of the 21st International Conference on Data Engineering (ICDE).
Discusses database optimizations, middleware, and the shift toward specialized AI-driven query systems.

Middleware & Edge Computing References

Kasselman, S. (2021). Designing Middleware for Distributed Systems. O'Reilly Media.

Examines middleware's role in enabling AI queries, security, and optimization.

Shi, W., Cao, J., Zhang, Q., Li, Y., & Xu, L. (2016). Edge Computing: Vision and Challenges. IEEE Internet of Things Journal.
Describes how edge computing improves AI-driven query performance and reduces latency.

Gubbi, J., Buyya, R., Marusic, S., & Palaniswami, M. (2013). Internet of Things (IoT): A Vision, Architectural Elements, and Future Directions. Future Generation Computer Systems.
Details the role of middleware in managing AI queries within IoT ecosystems.

AI Query Processing & Optimization References

Chollet, F. (2021). Deep Learning with Python (2nd ed.). Manning Publications.
Provides insight into neural networks and their application in AI query processing.

Dean, J., & Ghemawat, S. (2008). MapReduce: Simplified Data Processing on Large Clusters. Communications of the ACM.
Outlines large-scale query processing techniques used in AI-driven systems.

Mikolov, T., Sutskever, I., Chen, K., Corrado, G., & Dean, J. (2013). Distributed Representations of Words and Phrases and Their Compositionality. Advances in Neural Information Processing Systems (NeurIPS).

Introduces word embeddings and semantic search methodologies for AI queries.

Case Studies & Real-World Applications

Devlin, J., Chang, M.-W., Lee, K., & Toutanova, K. (2019). BERT: Pre-training of Deep Bidirectional Transformers for Language Understanding. Explores transformer-based models used in AI query engineering and NLP applications.

Halevy, A., Norvig, P., & Pereira, F. (2009). The Unreasonable Effectiveness of Data. IEEE Intelligent Systems.
Discusses data-driven approaches to AI and query optimization techniques.

Jeffery, S. R., Franklin, M. J., & Halevy, A. (2008). Pay-as-you-go User Feedback for Dataspace Systems. Proceedings of the ACM SIGMOD International Conference on Management of Data.
Examines user-driven query refinement and middleware feedback mechanisms.

Additional Online Resources

Google AI Research Blog (https://ai.googleblog.com/)
Regular updates on AI, machine learning, and advancements in query engineering.

MIT Computer Science and Artificial Intelligence Laboratory (CSAIL) (https://www.csail.mit.edu/)
Research publications related to AI middleware, neural networks, and

query optimizations.

O'Reilly AI Learning Platform (https://www.oreilly.com/ai/)
Courses, books, and hands-on tutorials on AI-driven middleware and AI
query techniques.

Summary

This bibliography provides a comprehensive reference list of books,
research papers, and online resources that underpin the methodologies
and best practices discussed in the AI Query Engineering Guide. These
references offer additional depth for readers seeking to explore advanced
topics in AI query optimization, middleware, neural networks, and edge
computing.

Index

Epilog

To My Readers, As we reach the conclusion of this AI Query Engineering Guide, it's important to reflect on the journey we have taken together. Throughout this guide, you have explored the foundational principles, methodologies, and advanced techniques that define the role of an AI Query Engineer. From understanding middleware as the speed layer to leveraging natural language querying and structured data retrieval, you have gained insights into a field that is rapidly shaping the future of AI-driven industries.

However, this guide is not an endpoint—it is a launchpad. AI will continue to evolve at an unprecedented pace, and the skills of an AI Query Engineer must evolve with it. Continuous learning, experimentation, and adaptation will be your most valuable tools as you refine your expertise and tackle new challenges in the field.

The demand for professionals who can bridge the gap between data, AI, and decision-making is growing. Those who master Query Engineering will not only be at the forefront of this movement but will help shape the next generation of AI applications and business intelligence.

Whether you are just beginning your journey or enhancing an already established career, I hope this guide has provided you with clarity, direction, and the confidence to engage with AI systems effectively. I hope you found this book to be a good source of information in the exciting world of AI.

Whether you liked the book or not, please leave a review—thank you.

Index

AI (Artificial Intelligence)

AI Query Engineer

Notes

www.ingramcontent.com/pod-product-compliance
Lightning Source LLC
Chambersburg PA
CBHW071302050326
40690CB00011B/2502